...ing bell. Across the snow, ...

...here joy and laughter dwell.

...ld be one thing and that one...

...g world and love's great m...

...heart in candle's glow and...

...e lights the way to hearth an...

...t we are and what we hope...

...t would be Christmas Eve...

...Christmas...

Rachel Mikels

PRESENTED TO

Krista M. Ross

FROM

November 26, 2001

DATE

Poems for Christmas

EXPRESSIONS OF JOY

WATERCOLORS BY
GAIL ROTH

IDEALS PUBLICATIONS, A DIVISION OF GUIDEPOSTS
NASHVILLE, TENNESSEE
WWW.IDEALSPUBLICATIONS.COM

ISBN 0-8249-4193-4

Caseside printed in the U.S.A.
Text printed and bound in Mexico.
Printed by R.R. Donnelley & Sons.

Published by Ideals Publications, a division of Guideposts
535 Metroplex Drive, Suite 250
Nashville, Tennessee 37211

Library of Congress Cataloging-in-Publication Data
Poems for Christmas: expressions of joy/ [Elizabeth Bonner Kea, editor].
    p. cm.
  ISBN 0-8249-4193-4
  1. Christmas—Poetry. 2. Christmas—Quotations, maxims, etc.
  I. Kea, Elizabeth, 1976–
PN6110.C5 P55 2000
808.81'9334—dc21   00-027772

10 8 6 4 2   3 5 7 9

POEMS SELECTED BY ELIZABETH BONNER KEA
DESIGNED BY EVE DEGRIE

ACKNOWLEDGMENTS

FARJEON, ELEANOR. "In the Week When Christmas Comes" from *Poems for Children*. Reprinted by permission of Harold
Ober Associates Incorporated. Copyright © 1927, 1955 by Eleanor Farjeon. GUEST, EDGAR. "The First Christmas Eve"
from *Living the Years* by Edgar Guest. Used with permission of the estate of Edgar Guest. RICHARDSON, ISLA PASCHAL.
"Christmas Eve—Christmas Morn." Used by permission of Branden Books. Our sincere thanks to the following authors
whom we were unable to locate: Mary C. Adams for "While My Heart Listens," Vic Jameson for "Three Gifts," Evelyn M.
Johnston for "Song of Isaiah," Marguerite Merington for "Christmas Eve," Alice Meynell for "Unto Us a Son is Given,"
Helen Welshimer for "Not Forgotten."

CONTENTS

THE MIRACLE OF CHRISTMAS 6

THE JOY OF CHRISTMAS 24

THE MUSIC OF CHRISTMAS 42

THE GIFTS OF CHRISTMAS 54

THE LOVE OF CHRISTMAS 68

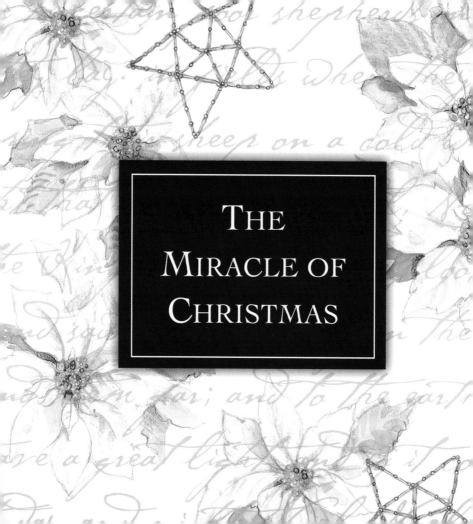

THE
MIRACLE OF
CHRISTMAS

WHILE MY HEART LISTENS

My eyes delight in every dear familiar touch
Of Christmas in the house—the pine, the silver bells,
And all the rest. But let them not rejoice in these too much
Lest they miss seeing angels as their chorus swells
In adoration of the Child whose house was bare
Except that love beyond all other love was there.

Let me not fret for baubles lacking for the tree,
At cookies to be baked and bundles left untied;
Nor mind the cluttered rooms, but sweep my spirit free
Of any pettiness, so He may come inside.
Let me forget all small and unimportant things
While my heart listens for the sound of angel wings.

—MARY C. ADAMS

As Joseph Was A-walking,

As Joseph was a-walking,
He heard an angel sing,
"This night shall be the birth-time
Of Christ, the heavenly king.

"He neither shall be born
In housen nor in hall,
Nor in the place of Paradise,
But in an ox's stall.

"He neither shall be clothed
In purple nor in pall,
But in the fair white linen
That usen babies all.

"He neither shall be rocked
In silver nor in gold,
But in a wooden manger
That resteth on the mould."

As Joseph was a-walking,
There did an angel sing,
And Mary's child at midnight
Was born to be our King.

Then be ye glad, good people,
This night for all the year,
And light ye up your candles,
For His star it shineth clear.

— TRADITIONAL ENGLISH CAROL

O Little Town of Bethlehem

O little town of Bethlehem,
How still we see thee lie,
Above thy deep and dreamless sleep
The silent stars go by;
Yet in thy dark streets shineth
The everlasting Light;
The hopes and fears of all the years
Are met in thee tonight.

For Christ is born of Mary;
And gather'd all above,
While mortals sleep, the angels keep
Their watch of wond'ring love.

O morning stars, together
Proclaim the holy birth
And praises sing to God the King
And peace to men on earth.

How silently, how silently,
The wondrous gift is giv'n!
So God imparts to human hearts
The blessings of His heav'n.
No ear may hear His coming,
But in this world of sin,
Where meek souls will receive Him still
The dear Christ enters in.

—PHILLIPS BROOKS

CHRISTMAS COMES SOFTLY

Christmas comes softly to the waiting heart,
In candle's glow and star and ringing bell.
Across the snow, glad welcome lights the way
To hearth and home where joy and laughter dwell.

If what we are and what we hope to be
Could be one thing and that one thing be true,
It would be Christmas Eve—a waiting world—
And love's great miracle forever new.

—CAROL BESSENT HAYMAN

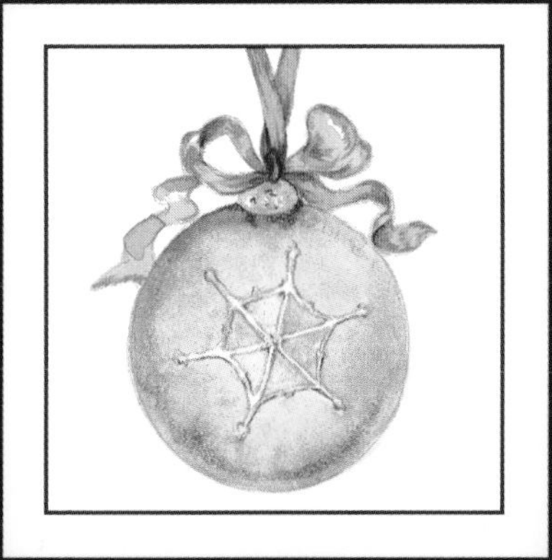

THREE GIFTS

God gave a child,
And in a manger lay the priceless gift of all eternity:
A sleeping babe, unheralded by rulers
    except for three
Who saw the everlasting hope of men
In a humble crib, in Bethlehem.

God gave a star
And by its light displayed a path
    for wandering shepherd folk to see
A Saviour child, unknown to millions
    heedless of the destiny
Of a soundless infant in repose,
Lying in a stall, in swaddling clothes.

God gave a song,
And angel legions sang
    the haunting phrases of a melody
That never ends and lifted from a tiny town's obscurity
A Boy-child born in a mound of hay
To give a waiting world its Christmas Day.
—VIC JAMESON

THE FIRST NOEL

The first Noel the angel did say,
Was to certain poor shepherds in fields as they lay:
In fields where they lay keeping their sheep
On a cold winter's night that was so deep.
Noel, Noel, Noel, Noel!
Born is the King of Israel.

They looked up and saw a star
Shining in the East beyond them far;
And to the earth it gave a great light,
And so it continued both day and night.
Noel, Noel, Noel, Noel!
Born is the King of Israel.

And by the light of that same star,
Three Wisemen came from country far;
To seek for a King was their intent,

And to follow the star, wherever it went.
Noel, Noel, Noel, Noel!
Born is the King of Israel.

This star drew nigh to the Northwest;
O'er Bethlehem it took its rest,
And there it did both stop and stay
    Right o'er the place where Jesus lay.
      Noel, Noel, Noel, Noel!
    Born is the King of Israel.

    Then entered in those Wisemen three,
    Full reverently upon their knee,
    And offered there, in His presence,
Their gold and myrrh and frankincense.
Noel, Noel, Noel, Noel!
Born is the King of Israel

—TRADITIONAL ENGLISH CAROL

POEMS FOR CHRISTMAS

The First Christmas Eve

Only a stable and straw for her bed,
And no one to notice the star overhead;
And only poor shepherds the Christ-child to see,
Who had heard that a cradle His manger would be.

How strangely God's purpose is hidden from men!
They were merely two travel-worn wanderers then.
Just Joseph and Mary in pitiful plight,
A stall in a stable her chamber that night.

No heralds with trumpets the Prince to receive,
No welcome by cannon that first Christmas Eve,
Just Joseph and Mary, with straw for her bed:
A Babe in a manger, a star overhead.
— Edgar A. Guest

JESUS OUR BROTHER

Jesus our brother, strong and good,
Was humbly born in a stable rude,
And the friendly beasts around Him stood,
Jesus our brother, strong and good.

"I," said the donkey, shaggy and brown,
"I carried His mother up hill and down,
I carried her safely to Bethlehem town,
I," said the donkey, shaggy and brown.

"I," said the cow, all white and red,
"I gave Him my manger for a bed;
I gave Him my hay to pillow His head.
I," said the cow, all white and red.

"I," said the sheep with curly horn,
"I gave Him my wool for His blanket warm,
He wore my coat on Christmas morn.
I," said the sheep with curly horn.

"I," said the dove, from the rafters high,
"Cooed Him to sleep that He should not cry;
We cooed Him to sleep, my mate and I.
I," said the dove from the rafters high.

Thus every beast by some good spell,
In the stable dark was glad to tell,
Of the gift he gave Emmanuel,
The gift he gave Emmanuel.
— TWELFTH CENTURY CAROL

CAROL

Villagers all, this frosty tide,
Let your doors swing open wide,
Though wind may follow, and snow beside,
Yet draw us in by your fire to bide;
Joy shall be yours in the morning!

Here we stand in the cold and sleet,
Blowing fingers, stamping feet,

Come from faraway you to greet—
You by the fire and we in the street—
Bidding you joy in the morning!

Goodman Joseph toiled through the snow—
Saw the star o'er a stable low;
Mary she might not further go—
Welcome thatch, and litter below!
Joy was hers in the morning!

And then they heard the angels tell,
"Who was first to cry Nowell?"
Animals all, as it befell,
In the stable where they did dwell!
"Joy shall be theirs in the morning!"
—Kenneth Grahame

THE
JOY OF
CHRISTMAS

RISE, HAPPY MORN

Rise, happy morn; rise, holy morn;
Draw forth the cheerful day from night:
O Father, touch the east,
And light the light that shone when
Hope was born.

—ALFRED, LORD TENNYSON

HOW JOYFULLY

Oh, how joyfully; Oh, how merrily,
Christmas comes with its grace divine!
Grace again is beaming,
Christ the world redeeming:
Hail, ye Christians,
Hail the joyous Christmastime!

—J. FALK

JOY TO THE WORLD

Joy to the world! the Lord is come;
Let earth receive her King;
Let ev'ry heart prepare Him room,
And heav'n and nature sing
And heav'n and nature sing
And heav'n and heav'n and nature sing.

Joy to the earth! the Saviour reigns;
Let men their songs employ;
While fields and floods, rocks, hills,
    and plains,
Repeat the sounding joy,

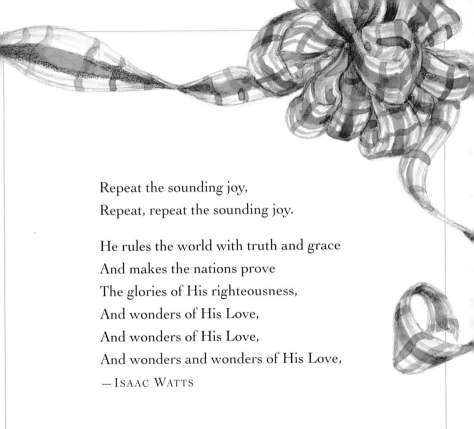

Repeat the sounding joy,
Repeat, repeat the sounding joy.

He rules the world with truth and grace
And makes the nations prove
The glories of His righteousness,
And wonders of His Love,
And wonders of His Love,
And wonders and wonders of His Love,
—ISAAC WATTS

'TIS MERRY 'NEATH THE MISTLETOE

'Tis merry 'neath the mistletoe,
When holly berries glisten bright;
When Christmas fires gleam and glow,
When wintry winds so wildly blow,
And all the meadows round are white —
'Tis merry 'neath the mistletoe!

A privilege 'tis then, you know,
To exercise time-honored rite;
When Christmas fires gleam and glow,
When loving lips may pout, although

With other lips they oft unite —
'Tis merry 'neath the mistletoe!

— JOSEPH ASHBY STERRY

The Holly and the Ivy

The holly and the ivy,
  Now they are full well-grown,
    Of all the trees that are in the wood,
    The holly bears the crown.

  The holly bears a blossom,
As white as the lily flower,
And Mary bore sweet Jesus Christ
To be our sweet Saviour.
— Medieval English Carol

DECK THE HALLS

Deck the halls with boughs of holly,
Fa la la la la, la la la la.
'Tis the season to be jolly,
Fa la la la la, la la la la.

Don we now our gay apparel,
Fa la la la la, la la la la.
Troll the ancient Yuletide carol,
Fa la la la la, la la la la.

See the blazing Yule before us,
Fa la la la la, la la la la.
Strike the harp and join the chorus,
Fa la la la la, la la la la.

Follow me in merry measure,
Fa la la la la, la la la la.
While I tell of Christmas treasure.
Fa la la la la, la la la la.

—WELSH CAROL

POEMS FOR CHRISTMAS

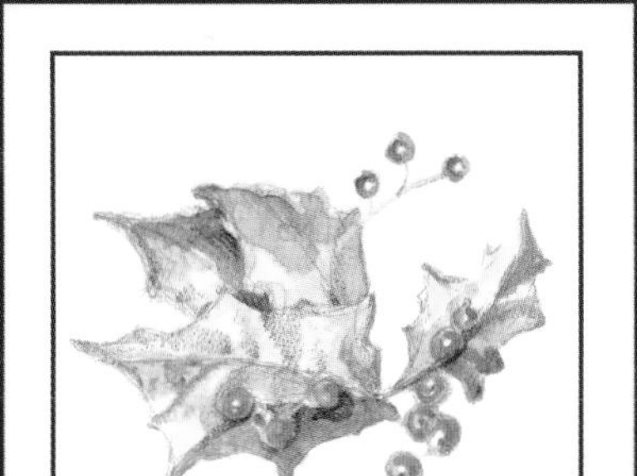

CHRISTMASTIME

Now that the time has come wherein
Our Saviour Christ was born,
The larder's full of beef and pork,
The granary's full of corn.

As God hath plenty to thee sent,
Take comfort of thy labors,
And let it never thee repent,
To feast thy needy neighbors.

—AUTHOR UNKNOWN

THE JOY OF GIVING

Somehow, not only for Christmas
But all the year through,
The joy that you give to others
Is the joy that comes back to you;
And the more you spend in blessing
The poor and lonely and sad,
The more of your heart's possessing
Returns to make you glad.

—JOHN GREENLEAF WHITTIER

OUR JOYFUL FEAST

So, now is come our joyful feast,
Let every soul be jolly!
Each room with ivy leaves is drest,
And every post with holly.

Though some churls at our mirth repine,
Round your brows let garlands twine,
Drown sorrow in a cup of wine,
And let us all be merry!

Now all our neighbors' chimneys smoke,
And Christmas logs are burning;
Their ovens with baked meats do choke,
And all their spits are turning.

Without the door let sorrow lie,
And if for cold it hap to die,
We'll bury it in Christmas pie,
And evermore be merry!
—GEORGE WITHER

POEMS FOR CHRISTMAS

THE CHRISTMAS FEAST

Now Christmas is come,

Let's beat up the drum,

And call all our neighbors together.

And when they appear,

Let us make them such cheer,

As will keep out the wind and the weather.

— WASHINGTON IRVING

CHRISTMAS TREES

I saw along each noisy city street
The trees for Christmas, standing dark and still;
The pines and firs come down from field and hill,
Old trees and young that had known sun and sleet.

Soft needles fell on hard, dull pavement there,
And forests rose in a most treeless place;
And there was gladness in each passing face,
And there was balsam fragrance everywhere.

Oh, lovely way to celebrate Your birth,
Whose birth star glistened through Judea's trees,
Whom Joseph taught the skillful use of these,
Who, on a Tree, once overcame the earth!

Grant then Your blessing, Friend of Trees, we pray,
On those who deck green boughs for Christmas Day!
— Violet Alleyn Storey

THE WEEK WHEN CHRISTMAS COMES

This is the week when Christmas comes.
Let every pudding burst with plums,
And every tree bear dolls and drums,
In the week when Christmas comes.

Let every hall have boughs of green
With berries glowing in between,
In the week when Christmas comes.

Let every doorstep have a song
Sounding the dark street along,
In the week when Christmas comes.

Let every night put forth a star
To show us where the heavens are,
In the week when Christmas comes.

Let every stable have a lamb
Sleeping warm beside its dam,
In the week when Christmas comes.
This is the week when Christmas comes.

—ELEANOR FARJEON

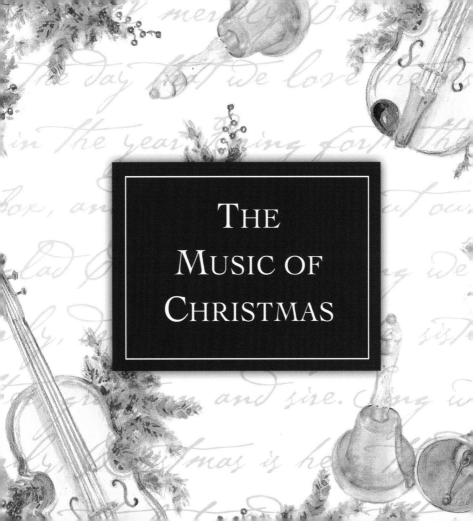

THE
MUSIC OF
CHRISTMAS

RING THE BELLS

Ring the bells, ring the bells,
Ring the merry Christmas bells!

And let their voice resound
    Around, around,
Till o'er the leas and o'er the fells
The gladsome echo gladly tells
How we today are blithe and gay,
And how for all sad hearts we pray.

Ring the bells, ring the bells,
Ring the joyful Christmas bells!
—ANNE LINDSAY BARNARD

THERE'S A SONG IN THE AIR!

There's a song in the air!
There's a star in the sky!
There's a mother's deep prayer
And a baby's low cry!
And the star rains its fire
While the beautiful sing,
For the manger of Bethlehem
   cradles a King.

There's a tumult of joy
O'er the wonderful birth,
For the Virgin's sweet Boy
Is the Lord of the earth.

Ay! the star rains its fire
While the beautiful sing,
For the manger of Bethlehem
    cradles a King!

We rejoice in the light,
And we echo the song
That comes down through the night
From the heavenly throng.
Ay! we shout to the lovely
Evangel they bring,
And we greet in His cradle,
    our Saviour and King!

—JOSIAH GILBERT HOLLAND

A CATCH BY THE HEARTH

Sing we all merrily, Christmas is here,
The day that we love the best of days in the year.
Bring forth the holly, the box, and the bay,
Deck out our parlor for glad Christmas-day.

Sing we all merrily, draw round the fire,
Sister and brother, grandson and sire.
Sing we all merrily, Christmas is here,
The day that we love the best of days in the year.

—AUTHOR UNKNOWN

SONG OF GREAT JOY

Sound over all waters, reach out from all lands,
The chorus of voices, the clasping of hands;
Sing hymns that were sung by the stars of the morn;
Sing songs of the angels when Jesus was born!

With glad jubilations
Bring hope to the nations!
Rise, hope of the ages, arise like the sun;
All speech flow to music, all hearts beat as one!

Sing the song of great joy
That the angels began;
Sing of glory to God
And of good will to man!

—JOHN GREENLEAF WHITTIER

WHY DO BELLS FOR CHRISTMAS RING?

Why do bells for Christmas ring?
Why do little children sing?

Once a lovely shining star,
Seen by shepherds from afar,
Gently moved until its light
Made a manger's cradle bright.

There a darling baby lay
Pillowed soft upon the hay;
And its mother sang and smiled:
"This is Christ, the Holy Child!"

Therefore bells for Christmas ring,
Therefore little children sing.

—EUGENE FIELD

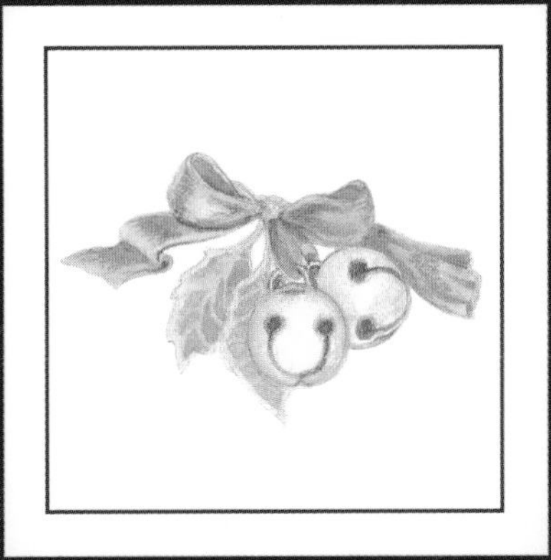

CHRISTMAS CAROL

Ring out, ye bells! All nature swells
With gladness of the wondrous story.
The world was torn but Christ is born
To change our sadness into glory.

Sing, earthlings, sing! Tonight a King
Hath come from heaven's high throne to bless us.
The outstretched hand o'er all the land
Is raised in pity to caress us.

Come at His call; be joyful all;
Away with mourning and with sadness!
The heavenly choir with holy fire
Their voices raise in songs of gladness.

The darkness breaks and dawn awakes,
Her cheeks suffused with youthful blushes.
The rocks and stones in holy tones
Are singing sweeter than the thrushes.

Then why should we in silence be
When nature lends her voice to praises,
When heaven and earth proclaim the truth
Of Him for whom that lone star blazes?

No, be not still, but with a will
Strike all your harps and set them ringing;
On hill and heath let every breath
Throw all its power into singing.

— PAUL LAURENCE DUNBAR

CHRISTMAS BELLS

I heard the bells on Christmas day
Their old, familiar carols play,
    And wild and sweet
    The words repeat
Of peace on earth, good will to men!

And thought how, as the day had come,
The belfries of all Christendom
    Had rolled along
    The unbroken song
Of peace on earth, good will to men!

Till, ringing, singing on its way,
The world revolved from night to day,
    A voice, a chime,

A chant sublime,
Of peace on earth, good will to men!

And in despair I bowed my head:
"There is no peace on earth," I said,
    "For hate is strong,
    And mocks the song
Of peace on earth, good will to men!"

Then pealed the bells more loud and deep:
"God is not dead, nor doth He sleep;
    The wrong shall fail,
    The right prevail,
With peace on earth, good will to men!"
— HENRY WADSWORTH LONGFELLOW

THE GIFTS OF CHRISTMAS

THE GOLDEN CAROL

We saw the light shine out a-far,
On Christmas in the morning;
And straight we knew Christ's star it was,
Bright beaming in the morning;

Then did we fall on bended knee,
On Christmas in the morning;
And prais'd the Lord who'd let us see
His glory at its dawning.

—TRADITIONAL ENGLISH CAROL

SONG OF ISAIAH

"For unto us a child is born,
To us a Son is given."
And to earth on Christmas morn
God sent His Gift from heaven.

"The government shall be upon
His shoulder," strong to bear
The burdens of mankind since dawn
Of time and all its care.

"His name was 'Wonderful' to be!"
The name of matchless worth,
For unto Him would every knee
Of man be bowed on earth.

"Counsellor, the mighty God,
The everlasting Father" of
All children of the common sod
Who bring to Him their love.

"The Prince of Peace," all hail to Him,
Who born in cattle stall,
Now reigns on high, mid seraphim . . .
The sovereign Lord of all.

— EVELYN M. JOHNSTON

A CHRISTMAS GIFT

A Christmas gift love sends to thee,
'Tis not a gift that you may see,
Like frankincense or shining gold,
Yet 'tis a gift that you may hold.

If you are lacking bread and meat,
'Twill give you heavenly bread to eat,
If you are down-trod, e'en as Job,
'Twill dress you in a seamless robe.

The gift of love in Mary's eyes,
Looked down on Jesus with surprise,
That one so great should be so small,
To point the way for kings and all.

One heart of love can move the race;
One grain of truth can change earth's face:
A Bethlehem Babe, a shepherd's rod
Have lifted mankind up to God.

—CLARENCE HAWKES

CHRISTMAS EVE—CHRISTMAS MORN

Expectant, eager eyes were slow to yield
Themselves to slumber at the close of day,
Knowing that on Christmas morrow all could say,
"A Merry Christmas!" Gifts to be revealed
Beneath the festooned tree would bring to all
Gay, glad surprises. Parents tiptoe round
The house with busy, busy hands. No sound
Is heard except the eerie whistling call
Of night winds and the gentle swish of snow
Against the windowpanes . . . then night is gone,
And peals of laughter greet the light of dawn,
When children wake and run, their eyes aglow,
Group joyously around the tree and gaze
In wonder and enchantment . . . . this remains
The hour that every childhood-year retains,
A vivid, tender memory— always.

—ISLA PASCHAL RICHARDSON

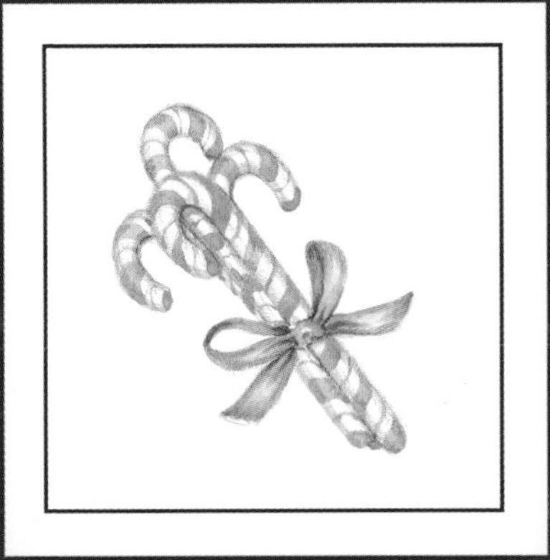

CHRISTMAS EVE

The children dreamed the whole night through
Of stockings hung the hearth beside;
And bound to make each dream come true
Went Santa Claus at Christmas-tide.

Black stockings, red, brown, white and gray —
Long, little, warm, or patched and thin —
The kindly saint found on his way
And, smiling, popped his presents in.

—MARGUERITE MERINGTON

GREETINGS FROM SANTA

He comes in the night! He comes in the night!
He softly, silently comes,
While the little brown heads on the pillows so white
Are dreaming of bugles and drums.
Who tells him I know not, but he findeth the home
Of each good little boy and girl.

He rides to the West, and he rides to the East;
Of his goodies, he touches not one;
He eats the crumbs of the Christmas feast
When the dear little folks are done.
Old Santa Claus does all that he can;
This beautiful mission is his;
Then children, be good to the little old man,
When you find who the little man is.

—AUTHOR UNKNOWN

A JOLLY LITTLE FELLOW

There's a jolly little fellow
Who comes riding into town,
When the North Wind blows his trumpet
And the snow comes dancing down.

In a coat of fur and ermine,
He is muffled to his chin;
And his face, whate'er the weather,
Always wears a pleasant grin.

He's a friend of all the children
For he carries on his back

Gifts to make the bright eyes sparkle,
Safely stowed within his pack;

And they always hang their stockings
By the fireplace because
Christmas Eve is sure to bring them
Presents from old Santa Claus.
—AUTHOR UNKNOWN

A STOCKING SONG

Welcome Christmas! heel and toe,
Here we wait thee in a row.
Come, good Santa Claus, we beg—
Fill us tightly, foot and leg.

Fill us quickly, 'ere you go;
Fill us till we overflow.
That's the way! and leave us more
Heaped in piles upon the floor.

Little feet that ran all day
Twitch in dreams of merry play;
Little feet that jumped at will
Lie all pink and warm and still.

See us, how we lightly swing;
Hear us, how we try to sing.
Welcome, Christmas, heel and toe,
Come and fill us 'ere you go.

Here we hang till someone nimbly
Jumps with treasure down the chimney.
Bless us! How he'll tickle us!
Funny old St. Nicholas!
— MARY MAPES DODGE

THE
LOVE OF
CHRISTMAS

When Christmas Comes

Have you any old grudges you would like to pay,
Any wrongs laid up from a bygone day?
Gather them now and lay them away
When Christmas comes.

Hard thoughts are heavy to carry, my friend,
And life is short from beginning to end;
Be kind to yourself, leave nothing to mend
When Christmas comes.

— WILLIAM LYTLE

No Sweeter Thing

Life holds no sweeter thing than this—to teach
A little child the tale most loved on earth
And watch the wonder deepen in his eyes
The while you tell him of the Christ Child's birth,

The while you tell of shepherds and a song,
Of gentle, drowsy beasts and fragrant hay
On which that starlit night in Bethlehem
God's tiny Son and His young mother lay.

Life holds no sweeter thing than this—to tell
A little child, while Christmas candles glow,
The story of a Babe whose humble birth
Became the loveliest of truths we know.
— Adelaide Love

AWAY IN A MANGER

Away in a manger, no crib for His bed,
The little Lord Jesus lay down His sweet head;
The stars in the heavens look'd down where He lay;
The little Lord Jesus asleep on the hay.

The cattle are lowing, the poor Baby awakes;
But little Lord Jesus no crying He makes.
I love thee, Lord Jesus; look down from the sky,
And stay by my cradle till morning is nigh.

Be near me, Lord Jesus; I ask Thee to stay
Close by me forever, and love me I pray.
Bless all the dear children in Thy tender care,
And take us to heaven to live with Thee there.

— MARTIN LUTHER

CHRISTMAS CAROL

The earth has grown old with its burden of care,
But at Christmas it always is young.
The heart of the jewel burns lustrous and fair,
And its soul full of music breaks forth on the air,
When the song of the angels is sung.

It is coming, old earth; it is coming tonight,
On the snowflakes which cover thy sod.
The feet of the Christ Child fall gently and white,
And the voice of the Christ Child tells out with delight
That mankind are the children of God.

On the sad and the lonely, the wretched and poor,
That voice of the Christ Child shall fall;
And to every blind wanderer opens the door
Of a hope which he dared not to dream before,
With a sunshine of welcome for all.

The feet of the humblest may walk in the field
Where the feet of the holiest have trod;
This, this is the marvel to mortals revealed,
When the silvery trumpets of Christmas have pealed:
That mankind are the children of God.

— PHILLIPS BROOKS

IN MY HEART

Christmas is where you are; the chimes, the snow,
All making a setting for the heart aglow,
But Christmas is more subtle than all these:
Something beyond the shimmering of trees,
Something that reaches deep within the heart
To find your song, though we are far apart.

And if you hear my voice across the years,
Singing the song we both have learned through tears,
Know that it holds the faith deep-planted there,
Nourished by your own dream and our one prayer.
There must be miles between us, but a ray
Shines through the darkness, and we know the way.
For where you are, the Christmas star is bright;
And it is Christmas in my heart tonight.

—MARY E. LINTON

Not Forgotten

I shall place white candles
On every windowsill:
One to face the roadway
and one to light the hill;

For I have read a story
Which says there was no light
In any house in Bethlehem
That other Christmas night.

Oh, should He come a wanderer
This night, the Christ must see
That, when I hung the stockings
And trimmed the Christmas tree,

I turned a shining moment
From revelry and din,
To place a gracious welcome,
In case He passed my inn.

—HELEN WELSHIMER

HOMEWARD BOUND

My heart is homeward bound these days
Because it's Christmastime.
When I see windows gaily decked
And hear the carols chime,
When I meet parcel-laden folks
Returning smiles with smiles,
My heart goes winging straight across
The intervening miles

To home, to family, and to friends
That childhood days made dear,
To hometown streets where passersby
Greet one with welcoming cheer.
Though years go by and decades too,
Still I have always found
When Christmastime makes its approach
My heart is homeward bound.

—Virginia Blanck Moore

POEMS FOR CHRISTMAS

Incarnate Love

Love came down at Christmas,
    Love all lovely,
    Love divine;
Love was born at Christmas,
Star and angels gave the sign.

Worship we the Godhead,
    Love incarnate,
    Love divine;
Worship we our Jesus:
But wherewith for sacred sign?

Love shall be our token,
    Love be yours and
    Love be mine,
Love to God and all men,
Love for plea and gift and sign.

—Christina Rossetti

Unto Us a Son Is Given

Given, not lent,
But not withdrawn—once sent,
This Infant of mankind, this One,
Is still the little welcome Son.

New every year,
New born and newly dear,
He comes with tidings and a song,
The ages long, the ages long.

Even as the cold,
Keen winter grows not old;
As childhood is so fresh, foreseen;
And spring in the familiar green—

Sudden as sweet
Come the expected feet.
All joy is young and new all art,
And He too whom we have by heart.

—ALICE MEYNELL

CANDLELIT HEART

Somewhere across the winter world tonight
You will be hearing chimes that fill the air;
Christmas extends its all-enfolding light
Across the distance . . . something we can share.
You will be singing, just the same as I,
These old familiar songs we know so well,
And you will see these same stars in your sky
And wish upon that brightest one that fell.
I shall remember you and trim my tree,
One shining star upon the topmost bough;
I will hang wreaths of faith that all may see.
Tonight I glimpse beyond the here and now;
And all the years we must be apart,
I keep a candle lighted in my heart.
—MARY E. LINTON

Title Index

As Joseph Was A-walking, 8
Away in a Manger, 71
Candlelit Heart, 84
Carol, 22
Catch by the Hearth, A, 46
Christmas Bells, 52
Christmas Carol, 50
Christmas Comes Softly, 12
Christmas Eve, 62
Christmas Eve—Christmas Morn, 60
Christmas Feast, The, 37
Christmas Gift, A, 58
Christmastide, 81
Christmastime, 32
Christmas Trees, 38
Deck the Halls, 30
First Christmas Eve, The, 19
First Noel, The, 16
Golden Carol, The, 55
Greetings from Santa, 63
Holly and the Ivy, The, 29
Homeward Bound, 78
How Joyfully, 25
Incarnate Love, 81

In My Heart, 74
It Is Coming Tonight, 50
Jesus Our Brother, 20
Jolly Little Fellow, A, 64
Joy of Giving, The, 33
Joy to the World, 26
No Sweeter Thing, 70
Not Forgotten, 76
O Little Town of Bethlehem, 10
Our Joyful Feast, 34
Ring the Bells, 43
Rise, Happy Morn, 25
Song of Great Joy, 47
Song of Isaiah, 56
Stocking Song, A, 66
There's a Song in the Air!, 44
Three Gifts, 14
'Tis Merry 'Neath the Mistletoe, 28
Unto Us a Son Is Given, 82
Week When Christmas Comes, The, 40
When Christmas Comes, 69
While My Heart Listens, 7
Why Do Bells for Christmas Ring?, 48

First Line Index

A Christmas gift love sends to thee, 58
As Joseph was a-walking, he heard an angel sing, 8
Away in a manger, no crib for His bed, 71
Christmas comes softly to the waiting heart, 12
Christmas is where you are; the chimes, the snow, 74
Deck the halls with boughs of holly, 30
Expectant, eager eyes were slow to yield, 60
"For unto us a child is born," 56
Given, not lent, 82
God gave a child, 14
Have you any old grudges you would like to pay, 69
He comes in the night!, 63
I heard the bells on Christmas day, 52
I saw along each noisy city street, 38
I shall place white candles on every windowsill, 76
Jesus our brother, strong and good, 20
Joy to the world! the Lord is come, 26
Life holds no sweeter thing than this—to teach, 70
Love came down at Christmas, 81
My eyes delight in every dear familiar touch, 7
My heart is homeward bound these days, 78
Now Christmas is come, 37
Now that the time has come wherein, 32

Oh, how joyfully, oh, how merrily, 25
O little town of Bethlehem, how still we see thee lie, 10
Only a stable and straw for her bed, 19
Ring out, ye bells! all nature swells, 50
Ring the bells, ring the bells, 43
Rise, happy morn; rise, holy morn, 25
Sing we all merrily, Christmas is here, 46
Somehow, not only for Christmas, 33
Somewhere across the winter world tonight, 84
So, now is come our joyful feast, 34
Sound over all waters, reach out from all lands, 47
The children dreamed the whole night through, 62
The earth has grown cold with its burden of care, 72
The first Noel the angel did say, 16
The holly and the ivy, now they are full well grown, 29
There's a jolly little fellow, 64
There's a song in the air!, 44
This is the week when Christmas comes, 40
'Tis merry 'neath the mistletoe, 28
Villagers all, this frosty tide, 22
Welcome Christmas! heel and toe, 66
We saw the light shine out a-far, 55
Why do bells for Christmas ring?, 48

FIRST LINE INDEX

Author Index

Adams, Mary C., 7
Barnard, Anne Lindsay, 43
Brooks, Phillips, 10, 72
Dickens, Charles, 61
Dodge, Mary Mapes, 66
Dunbar, Paul Laurence, 50
Falk, J., 25
Farjeon, Eleanor, 40
Field, Eugene, 48
Grahame, Kenneth, 22
Guest, Edgar A., 19
Hawkes, Clarence, 58
Hayman, Carol Bessent, 12
Holland, Josiah Gilbert, 44
Irving, Washington, 37
Jameson, Vic, 14
Johnston, Evelyn M., 56
Linton, Mary E., 74, 84
Longfellow, Henry Wadsworth, 52
Lord Tennyson, Alfred, 25

Love, Adelaide, 70
Luther, Martin, 71
Lytle, William, 69
Marshall, Peter, 18
MacFerran, G., 36
Merington, Marguerite, 62
Meynell, Alice, 82
Moore, Virginia Blanck, 78
Richardson, Isla Paschal, 60
Rossetti, Christina, 81
Scott, Sir Walter, 31
Smith, Alexander, 13
Sterry, J. Ashby, 28
Storey, Violet Alleyn, 38
Watts, Issac, 26
Welshimer, Helen, 76
Wither, George, 34
Whittier, John Greenleaf, 33, 47
York, Esther Baldwin, 75

welcome lights the way to

want we are and what we

be true, it would be Chris

be forever new. Christmas co

and ringing bell. Across the

ome where joy and laughter

could be one thing and that

aiting world and love's gre

ing bell. Across the snow,

here joy and laughter dwell

ld be one thing and that on

world and love's great m

heart in candle's glow and

lights the way to hearth an

we are and what we hope

would be Christmas Eve